Irish Round Towers

Roger Stalley

Country House, Dublin

First published in 2000 by
Town House and Country House Ltd,
Trinity House, Charleston Rd
Ranelagh, Dublin 6
ISBN: 1-86059-114-0

Series editor: Dr Michael Ryan
Printed in Spain by Estudios Graficos ZURE

CONTENTS

THE DATE OF THE TOWERS   6

WHAT WERE ROUND TOWERS USED FOR?   10

BELLS AND BELFRIES   14

ORIGINS AND INFLUENCES   35

CONSTRUCTION FEATURES   36
Height and proportions
Corbelled roofs
Tapering profile
Construction methods

A NATIONAL ICON   43

SELECT BIBLIOGRAPHY   46

INDEX   47

TORY ISLAND

ARMOY

ANTRIM

RAM'S ISLAND

DRUMBO
NENDRUM

DRUMCLIFF
DEVENISH

KILLALA
CLONES

ARMAGH
MAGHERA
DOWNPATRICK

INISHKEEN

DRUMLANE
LOUTH
DROMISKIN

MEELICK
TURLOUGH
AGHAGOWER BALLA

MONASTERBOICE
KELLS
ARDBRACCAN
TULLAGHARD
TRIM
SLANE
DONAGHMORE
DULEEK
LUSK

ORAN
ROSCOMMON

KILBENNAN

KILCOONA
ANNAGHDOWN CLONMACNOISE
ROSCAM

CLONARD
SWORDS
DUBLIN
CLONDALKIN

TAGHADOE
OUGHTERARD

RATHMICHAEL

ARDRAHAN
KILMACDUAGH

SEIRKIERAN
ROSCREA

KILDARE
KILCULLEN
GLENDALOUGH

KILLEANY

KILLINABOY
DYSERT O'DEA
DRUMCLIFF

INISCEALTRA
TUAMGRAINEY

TIMAHOE

CASTLEDERMOT

SCATTERY

FERTAGH

LIATHMORE

KILKENNY
TULLAHERIN

DYSERT OENGHUSA

RATTOO

KILMALLOCK
ARDPATRICK

CASHEL
EMLY

KILREE

ST MULLINS

AGHAVILLER

AGHADOE

ARDMORE

KINNEIGH

CLOYNE

ROSS CARBERY

Freestanding Round Towers

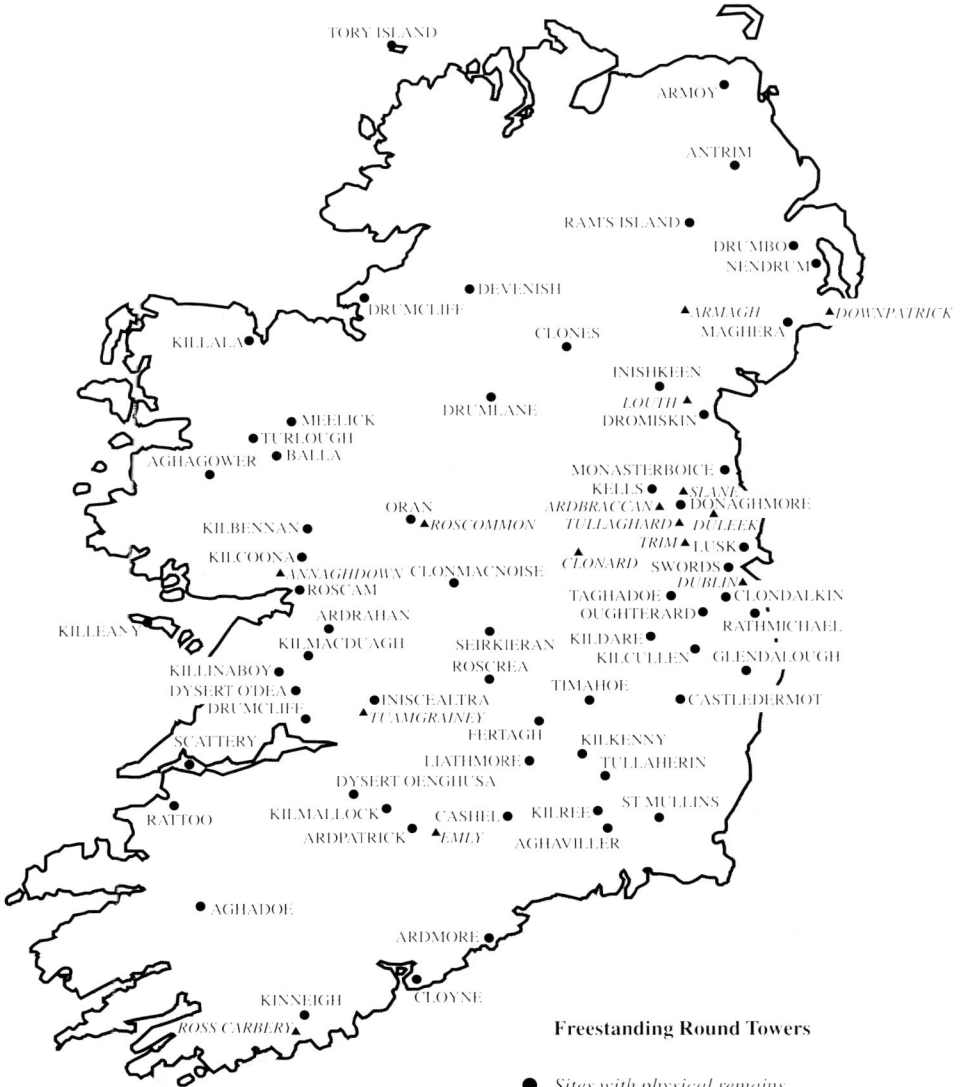

● *Sites with physical remains*
▲ *Sites where towers are known to have existed*

4

From Glendalough to Kilmacduagh, and from Tory island to Ardmore, so-called round towers punctuate the Irish landscape in a memorable and often dramatic way. We know of the existence of over eighty examples, though it is likely that there were once many more, perhaps over a hundred in the country as a whole. While some have been restored, many survive as ruins, and a few are known only from historical sources.

Round towers were normally erected as free-standing structures, built as great tubes of stone, extending upwards ninety or one hundred feet (Pl 1). A single doorway provided the only means of access and this was usually placed well above the ground (Photos 1, 2). Inside, the vertical space of the tower was divided into several storeys by wooden floors, some of which have been reinstated in modern times. To reach the top it was necessary to climb a series of steep ladders from floor to floor.

The final storey, which was generally illuminated by four windows, was covered by a conical roof of stone, built on the ancient corbelled system. These conical caps provide a splendid finale to the design, anticipating the stone spires of the Gothic age (Photo 3). Seen from a distance, round towers have a natural elegance, a quality derived from a gradual reduction in diameter as the tower increases in height.

*Photo 1
Monasterboice
(Louth) with its
crosses and round
tower as depicted
in a lithograph
from O'Neill's*
The Most
Interesting of
the Sculptured
Crosses of
Ancient Ireland
*(1857). (Board of
Trinity College,
Dublin)*

5

THE DATE OF THE TOWERS

A rough chronology of the towers can be established by a study of the Irish annals. The first reference to a *cloigtheach* (literally, bell-house) comes in about AD 950, with the burning of a tower at Slane, and this is followed by references to towers

6

elsewhere, in 964, 981 and 995–6. It is evident, therefore, that the concept of the round tower was introduced to Ireland at some point during the first half of the tenth century. The last (medieval) reference to the construction of a tower comes in 1238, at Annaghdown (Galway). This means that we have a three-hundred-year span of building, from the early tenth to the early thirteenth century.

In a few instances it is possible to offer more precise dates. The annals tell us that a tower at Monasterboice was burnt in 1097, and, as the existing tower contains no trace of damage, it was probably built soon after the fire (Photo 1). More exact evidence survives for the tower at Clonmacnoise, finished in 1124 under the auspices of abbot Gillachrist Ua Maoileoin and king Toirrdelbach Ua Conchobair (Turlough O'Connor) (Pl 2). Like the towers at Ardmore and Timahoe, this is constructed in well-dressed ashlar masonry, characteristic of the twelfth century. The quality of the masonry can sometimes provide chronological clues, though the use of rough rubble rather than ashlar is not necessarily an indication of a pre-1100 date (Pl 3). At both Clonmacnoise and Drumlane, excellent ashlar low down in the tower is followed by much coarser work above.

The existence of local quarries and the nature of the geological environment could affect the style of masonry. Thus at Castledermot the tower is made from rounded boulders of granite, while at Kilmacduagh the lower sections of the tower are constructed with huge slabs of stone, set on edge, and finished with very precise joints. The latter is generally described as 'megalithic' or 'cyclopean' masonry, a technique which can be paralleled in a number of early Irish churches (Pl 3).

As well as distinctions in masonry, there are other clues which can help to establish a date. Several towers are embellished with Romanesque ornament, which came into vogue during the second quarter of the twelfth century. The towers at

Photo 3 Cashel (Tipperary). Built of well dressed masonry, the tower was probably erected soon after the site was handed over to the church in 1101. The head of the triangular window is formed from a single block of stone. The cap was rebuilt in the 1870s. (Dúchas, The Heritage Service)

7

Photo 4 Timahoe (Laois). The tower is entered through an ornate doorway, embellished with chevron patterns and grotesque heads, sculptured in a style characteristic of Hiberno-Romanesque.

Photo 5 Devenish (Fermanagh). One of four sculptured heads that decorate the string course at the base of the cap. The tower was erected in the second half of the twelfth century. (British Crown copyright. Reproduced with the permission of the Controller of Her Majesty's Stationery Office)

8

Timahoe (Laois) and Kildare, for example, have Romanesque decoration around the doorways, and at Devenish (Fermanagh) there are Romanesque corbel heads below the cap (Photos 4, 5).

In fact a considerable number of the remaining towers appear to belong to the twelfth century, though some of these may be replacements for earlier towers. This was certainly true at Devenish, where excavations only a few feet from the surviving Romanesque tower have revealed the foundations of its predecessor (Pl 4b). This earlier building may have been damaged or destroyed in 1176, when there is a record of a king of Fermanagh being burned inside a tower at Devenish. The existing tower could have been constructed as a replacement shortly afterwards.

Differences in the design of doors and windows offer further chronological hints (Pl 6). There are over a dozen doorways which are covered by lintels, and it is tempting to regard these as somewhat earlier than arched doorways. When arches were employed, they were frequently constructed using only two or three stones. In some cases false arches were made by cutting a curved section from the underside of a lintel. Twelfth-century towers with Romanesque decoration (Devenish, Donaghmore, Kildare, Timahoe, Dysert Oenghus, Dromiskin and Ardmore) have arched doorways, which implies that the arch was a late development.

A number of tower doors are surrounded by a raised band carved in the adjoining stonework, echoing the strip work found in Anglo-Saxon churches from around the year 1000. Examples can be found in the towers at Monasterboice, Rattoo, Roscrea, Cashel and Donaghmore (Photo 6). Another technique with Anglo-Saxon parallels is the use of triangular-headed windows, formed by setting two stones against each other at an angle.

Photo 6 Rattoo (Kerry). The round-headed doorway is built of well-dressed masonry. The arch is made from three blocks, which are decorated with barely visible curvilinear ornament; a thin raised band surrounds the doorway, accentuating its shape. (Dúchas, The Heritage Service)

WHAT WERE ROUND TOWERS USED FOR?

During the nineteenth century, the purpose of the towers was the focus of much speculation and eccentric theorising. According to one view, they were fire temples, the idea being that they were designed for sun worship, with a fire kept perpetually burning at the summit. Then there was the notion that they were intended for celestial observations by the druids, functioning, it was supposed, as primitive astronomical observatories.

Photo 7 Dromiskin (Louth). The Romanesque doorway was composed of two separate orders of arches, the outer one resting on detached columns which are now lost.

Given their distinctive form, it was perhaps inevitable that some would see them as monuments to Priapus, a triumphant assertion of masculine virility. A certain Henry O'Brien, who was active in the middle years of the nineteenth century, insisted that they were relics of phallus worship, a cult supposedly brought to Ireland by Buddhist émigrés from India, who, he claimed, colonised the country in the pre-Christian era. In 1832 this gentleman was awarded a prize of £20 for his work by no less a body than the Royal Irish Academy, paid, one suspects, not to reward his endeavours but as an attempt to keep him quiet (Photo 8).

Already in the eighteenth century, many antiquaries had come to appreciate that the round towers were Christian buildings, though there was much dispute about

Photo 8 Henry O'Brien, engraved portrait after Daniel Maclise. O'Brien's eccentric opinions about round towers served to confuse the nineteenth century public and infuriated more sober scholars like George Petrie. (from H.O'Brien, The Round Towers of Ireland, second edition, London, 1898)

their precise purpose. Some argued that they were built by Irish followers of Symeon Stylites, the saint who spent his life in isolation at the top of a column. A variant of this interpretation was the penitential tower, the theory being that miscreants were sent to the top storey and allowed to descend floor by floor as they gradually fulfilled their penance. Others saw them as gnomons, with the towers functioning as the centre of giant sun dials, though no evidence of the dial itself was ever produced.

Investigations were placed on a more rational and sober footing in 1845 with the publication of a famous book by George Petrie, the distinguished artist, scholar and antiquary (Photo 9). Petrie demonstrated that the towers had an ecclesiastical origin and that they functioned as bell towers, a point confirmed by the Irish word *cloigtheach* or 'bell house'. He also showed that they were associated with monasteries, where the ringing of a bell was essential as a means of calling the monks to prayer at regular intervals throughout the day. Petrie's book was based on the text of an essay which he had submitted to the Royal Irish Academy in 1832, as part of a competition to explain the origin of the towers.

Although the more bizarre myths associated with round towers have long since been dispelled, there are still a number of questions that remain unanswered. We know nothing about the circumstances in which the towers were introduced to Ireland, nor the site of the first one to be built. It is generally assumed that the design was based on models elsewhere in Christian Europe, but there is no agreement about where these models might have been. Nor is it known what sort of bells were used in

Photo 9 Portrait of George Petrie by John Slattery (1857). Petrie was the first person to place the study of round towers on a rational and scholarly basis. (Royal Irish Academy)

11

*Photo 10
Kilmacduagh
(Galway). With
its distinctive
lean, this is the
Irish equivalent
of the famous
tower at Pisa.
The doorway is
over 25 feet above
the ground; a
rigid ladder of
this length could
not have been
pulled up into
the tower.*

12

the towers and how they were rung. The height of the towers and the raised doorways are further issues which demand an explanation.

The annals contain six references to people being killed in round towers, at times when they were being used as places of defence or escape. When the tower at Slane was burned by the Vikings in 950, a considerable number of people, crammed inside, died in the blaze. Precious relics, a crosier and 'a bell, the best of bells' were also destroyed. In 1076 Murchadh, son of Flann Ua Maelsechlainn, who had recently become king of Tara, was murdered in the tower at Kells, no doubt trying to escape from his enemies.

These incidents have encouraged the belief that the towers were designed, at least in part, as places of refuge. Indeed there is a widely held view that round towers were primarily defensive structures, and were valuable as 'look-outs', especially during the Viking invasions. It is assumed that in times of danger everyone in the monastery dashed for the tower and climbed up a ladder to the doorway. When all were safely inside, the ladder was pulled up and the door firmly locked.

But things were not quite so simple. In many cases, pulling up a ladder would have been a physical impossibility: at Kilmacduagh, for example, the door is so high that an external ladder would have been almost 30 feet long; only if it had been made of rubber or some other flexible material could it have been manipulated into the tower! (Photo 10). One scholar has suggested that rope ladders were employed, which conjures up a rather extraordinary picture of life in the early Irish monastery, with elderly monks scrambling up rope ladders at the first sign of danger, books and reliquaries under their arms. It does not seem a very plausible scenario.

The external ladder or steps must have been semi-permanent structures, probably designed with a platform outside the door (Pl 6a). In fact the occasional burning of the towers suggests that an aggressor with enough determination could reach the entry floor without too much difficulty. Once the door had been broken down, the attacker could burn the wooden floors, as happened at Slane in 950.

While round towers were certainly regarded as convenient hiding places, it is unlikely that defence was uppermost in the minds of the first builders. At best they provided a temporary refuge.

In a few cases the doorway was in any case close to ground level, which was curious if the towers were envisaged as defensive structures. There is an example on

13

Scattery Island, where the monastery was a sitting target, exposed to every band of marauders sailing up the Shannon estuary (Photo 19); it was ransacked at least five times in the two hundred years between 972 and 1176. Here was an instance where a raised doorway might have proved its value.

On balance, therefore, one can conclude that towers were constructed primarily for ringing bells, though this function did not preclude their use as hideouts during emergencies, or as safe places to store valuables.

BELLS AND BELFRIES

Bells were the clocks of the middle ages and the sound of a bell at regular intervals provided the framework for a well-ordered religious life. Thus saints and ecclesiastics were depicted in early Irish sculpture holding a bell as a mark of authority (Pl 7). For several centuries hand-bells seemed to have been rung from beside the church, but this practice began to change in the tenth century with the introduction of the round towers.

The advantage of a tower was that the sound of the bell travelled a greater distance, which suggests that monks were having difficulty picking up the sound. This was a serious issue, for we know that those who arrived late at the daily offices were liable to be punished. The rule of St Columbanus makes it clear that failure to hear the bell was not accepted as an excuse for late attendance. Hearing the bell must have become more difficult as monasteries grew larger and the noise levels increased. A tall campanile, which radiated the sound over a wide range, was thus a convenient way of maintaining order at a time when

Photo 11 Iniscealtra (Clare). Situated on an island in Lough Derg. Iniscealtra became an important centre of pilgrimage. The location of the tower, to the south-west or north-west of the main church, was a standard arrangement.

ecclesiastical settlements were becoming more like towns or cities.

The towers also had a symbolic value, providing a permanent reminder of the discipline of monastic life. In several instances there was a clear association between the tower and the major church of the monastery (Photo 11). At Glendalough and Clonmacnoise, for example, the tower is situated a short distance to the north-west of the cathedral, with the doorway pointing towards the main entrance of the church. In other cases, however, the tower was much closer. At Tullaherin (Tullamaine) in 1121 a stone falling from the tower during a thunder storm killed a student in the church, so presumably the two buildings were almost contiguous (Photo 12).

It is generally assumed that at appropriate times the *aistreoir* or bell ringer climbed up the tower and rang a hand-bell out of each of the four windows. While this might be true, it is odd that Irish monasteries put their bell ringer to so much trouble; if a bell was rung from the tower at the start of each of the daily offices, the *aistreoir* would have had to climb 700 feet every day, almost 5000 feet each week.

Elsewhere in Europe monastic officials avoided such physical labour by using bell ropes. Notker, for example, tells a story about a craftsman named Tancho from St Gall who cast a bell for the Emperor Charlemagne. He tried to cheat the emperor by substituting tin for silver in the alloy, and when the bell was eventually hung in the bell-tower, nobody could make it ring. Tancho 'seized hold of the rope and tugged at the bell', whereupon it broke free from its frame and crashed to the ground, hitting the unfortunate Tancho *en route* and 'taking his bowels and testicles with it'. Notker wrote his *Life* about AD 883–7 and he writes as if what he says about bells was a perfectly normal arrangement.

Photo 12 Tullaherin (Kilkenny). This monastic site, otherwise known as Tullamaine, was struck by lightning in 1121, when a stone fell from the tower, killing a student in the church. The belfry windows were remade in the later middle ages. (Dúchas, The Heritage Service)

Bell ropes were known from at least the sixth century and there is a famous painting in a Spanish manuscript which shows a multi-storeyed belfry, with a bell ringer using ropes to sound the two bells suspended in turrets at the top (Pl 12). This dates from 970.

Why, therefore, did the Irish not adopt the same solution? Is it possible that larger bells were hung permanently at the top of the towers and operated by ropes?

At first sight there seems to be little evidence to support this. Over seventy Irish bells survive but all are hand-bells and there is not a single example of a larger bell such as might be hung in a wooden frame (Pl 7b). Given the size of this collection, it is odd that no large bells survive, if indeed they were manufactured for the early Irish church.

The vast majority of the hand-bells belong to the period 700–900 and there are very few bells that can be assigned to the twelfth century with any confidence. For some reason hand-bells seem to have gone out of fashion after 900, at the very period when the round towers began to appear on the landscape.

Having gone to the trouble and expense of building huge campaniles, it would be remarkable if new and larger bells were not commissioned at the same time. None, however, survive. There might be a good reason for this. Many of the round towers remained in use as belfries during the later middle ages, so their bells never became redundant like the early hand-bells; when a bell was cracked or damaged, it was simply recast, especially if it was made of bronze. Bell metal was just too valuable to waste. (Its value was demonstrated in 1552, when the English garrison of Athlone seized the 'large bells' from the *cloigtheach* of Clonmacnois, no doubt with the intention of re-using the metal for military purposes.)

Although there is no archaeological evidence for bell frames at the top of the round towers, there is documentary evidence that ropes were in use in Ireland, at least in the twelfth century. One of the privileges given to the abbey of Cong by Rory O Conor, king of Connacht (1156–98) was the right to receive a bell rope from every ship coming to the port of Cill Mór for fishing and trading. Moreover, a rope must have been used at St Kevin's church at Glendalough, where there is a tiny round bell turret, in effect a miniature round tower (Pl 13a). Nobody could have been expected to scramble into the turret every time the bell had to be rung.

16 *cont. p.33*

Pl 1 Glendalough
(Wicklow).
Constructed as
a giant cylinder
of stone, this
rubble built tower
is almost 100
feet high.

17

*Pl 2
Clonmacnoise
(Offaly). The
tower was
finished in 1124
but within eleven
years it had
been damaged
by lightning.
The angle of
diminution
changes sharply
at the level of the
doorway, most
noticeably on the
left side of the
tower.*

18

The masonry of the round towers: Pl 3a Glendalough (Wicklow). Probably eleventh century: coursed rubble masonry made up of local mica-schist and some granite; note the offset at the base of the tower, which is a common feature.

Pl 3b Clonmacnoise (Offaly), 1124. Well-dressed sandstone blocks with the face of the stones cut to a slight curve.

Pl 3c Kilmacduagh (Galway), an example of 'Cyclopean' masonry, where huge slabs were employed; although the shape of the stones is far from regular, the joints are remarkably precise.

19

Devenish
(Fermanagh):
Pl 4a
A tower at
Devenish was
burned in 1176
with the king of
Fermanagh
inside; the
surviving
Romanesque
tower with its
splendid ashlar
masonry may
have been
constructed as a
replacement for
the damaged
building.

Pl 4b
The foundations
of an earlier
tower lie in the
shadow of the
existing structure.

20

Pl 5 Clondalkin (Dublin). Built of roughly coursed calp (limestone), Clondalkin is one of the best preserved towers, with its original cap still in place. Now a suburb of Dublin, Clondalkin was the site of an early monastery.

21

Doorways:
Pl 6a Clondalkin
(Dublin). The
door is covered
by a lintel, made
of a large block
of granite. The
stone steps,
although added
later, may reflect
the arrangement
of the original
wooden stairs.

22

*Pl 6b
Glendalough
(Wicklow).
Although the door
appears to be
covered by an
arch, the curve
is in fact cut out
of a single block
of stone. As is
frequently the
case, the jambs
are inclined
inwards, a feature
of early Irish
architecture.*

*Pl 6c
Clonmacnoise
(Offaly). Although
the arch is
composed of
well cut voussoir
blocks, the jambs
are still inclined
inwards following
Irish tradition.*

23

Pl 7a White Island (Fermanagh). Ecclesiastical figure holding a bell and crosier, probably tenth century. Hand-bells were part of the insignia of ecclesiastical authority in the early church, but whether they were rung from the top of the towers remains an open question.

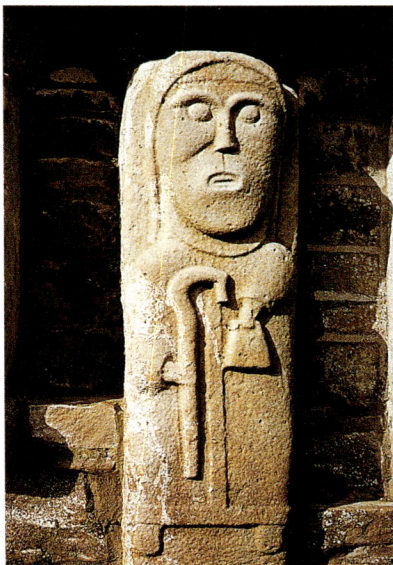

Pl 7b Hand-bell. Over seventy early hand-bells made from iron or bronze survive. (National Museum of Ireland)

24

*Pl 8 Donaghmore
(Meath). This
well preserved
tower is peculiar
since it lacks
belfry windows.
Although the
conical cap is
incomplete, the
remains appear
to be original.
The doorway is
surmounted by
a carving of the
crucifixion, as
in the tower at
Brechin (Angus).*

25

Pl 9a Antrim (Antrim). The rubble built tower may be one of the earliest examples to survive, dating perhaps from the late tenth or early eleventh century. Above its lintelled doorway, there is a stone decorated with a ringed cross. (British Crown copyright. Reproduced with the permission of the Controller of Her Majesty's Stationery Office)

Pl 9b Donaghmore (Meath). The triangular window, the head of which is formed by two stones, has many parallels in Anglo-Saxon architecture.

26

Pl 10 Swords (Dublin). Built of rubble masonry, the round tower at Swords belonged to a monastery said to have been founded by St Columba. The belfry stage and the conical cap were clumsily rebuilt either in the later middle ages or more recently.

27

Pl 11 Kilmacduagh (Galway). The tower is famous for its pronounced and irregular lean.

Pl 12. The Tavara Apocalypse c970. The Spanish illumination depicts a tower with two bell turrets. The bells are being rung by ropes held by a figure at the bottom. (Madrid, Archivo Histórico Nacional, cod. 1097B)

28

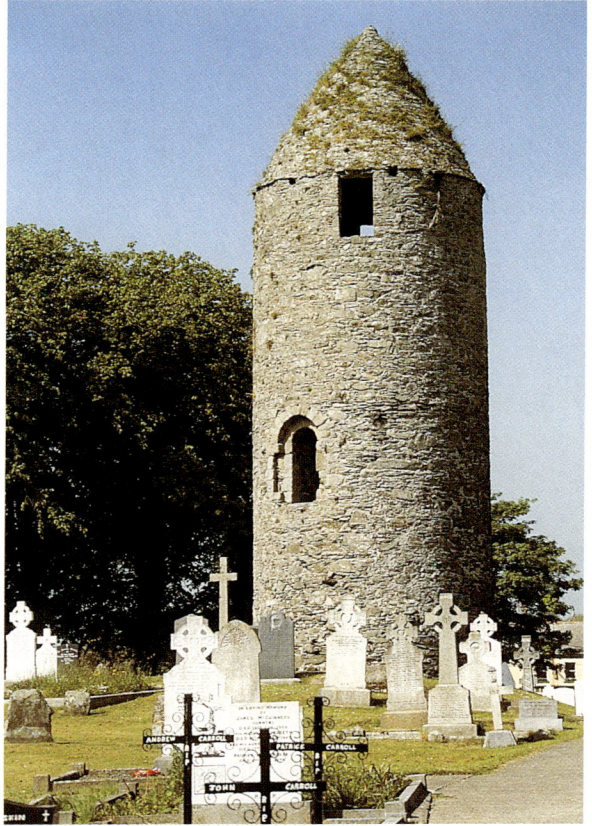

*Pl 13a
Glendalough
(Wicklow), St.
Kevin's Church.
This is one of
several Irish
churches with a
round tower
incorporated into
the fabric. In this
case the bell must
have been rung by
means of a rope.*

*Pl 13b Dromiskin
(Louth). At some
point in its history
the height of
the tower was
drastically
reduced, though
the original idea
of a conical roof
was retained.*

29

*Pl 14 Lusk
(Dublin). The
circular tower of
the early medieval
monastery (seen
on the left) was
incorporated into
a huge belfry
in the later
middle ages.*

Pl 15 Ravenna,
Sant'Apollinare
in Classe. This is
one of several
detached towers
at Ravenna that
have been
compared with
Irish examples.
With their tiled
roofs and
capacious
windows, the
design of the
Italian towers
is significantly
different from
those in Ireland.

31

Pl 16a Listowel, the Central Hotel (Kerry). Erin with her harp and greyhound, depicted alongside a round tower, which by this time had become a well established national symbol. (George Mott)

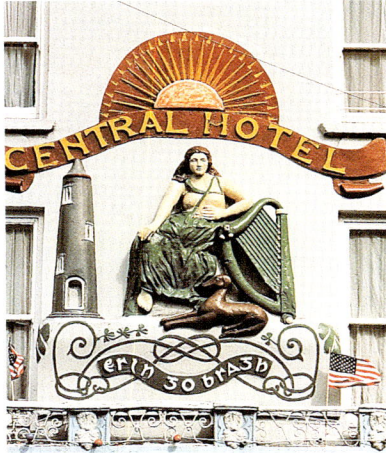

Pl 16b Glasnevin (Dublin). The O'Connell monument. Erected in 1869, this Dublin landmark was one element of the O'Connell memorial, which was designed to include a chapel and a high cross. George Petrie was consulted, though he took no responsibility for the height of the tower.

Pl 16c Dromore Castle (Limerick) 1867–70. Designed by E.W. Godwin for the third Earl of Limerick, this was one of several nineteenth-century country houses to incorporate a round tower on the ancient model.

32

cont. from p.16

It is also important to note that documentary sources suggest that bells came in two different sizes. A twelfth-century legal source, describing the duties of the *aistreoir*, asserts: 'Noble his work when the bell is that of a *cloigtheach*, humble his work when it is a hand-bell.' The bells of the *cloigtheach*, or round tower, were clearly different and evidently harder to ring. While the evidence is far from conclusive, one cannot exclude the possibility that bells were hung permanently at the top of the round towers and were operated by ropes.

In several cases round towers were incorporated into churches. At Glendalough, for example, a diminutive belfry projects from the roof of St Kevin's church like a chimney (Pl 13a), and until 1818 a circular tower survived at the west end of Trinity church nearby. A small, beautifully built round tower is attached to the south side of Temple Finghin at Clonmacnoise (Photo 13); old photographs and drawings show that the cap here was originally built with specially cut stones, arranged in a herringbone design.

Churches with their own belfry towers, while common in other countries of Europe, remained rare in Ireland until the Gothic age. The reason probably has something to do with scale. A round tower 100 feet high would have looked absurd had it been attached to one of the relatively small churches favoured by the early Irish monasteries.

Several round towers remained in use as belfries throughout the middle ages, and that at Cloyne still retains its bells. In three cases (Cloyne, Castledermot and Kildare) the conical roofs were replaced by medieval battlements. At Lusk the ancient tower was integrated into the angle of a late medieval tower, with three further turrets added at the other angles to provide a degree of symmetry (Pl 14). The resulting composition is one of the most imposing medieval sights in the country.

Photo 13 Clonmacnoise (Offaly). Temple Finghin which has a round tower attached beside the chancel. This old view reproduced from the Earl of Dunraven's book of 1875–6 clearly shows the 'herringbone' masonry of the cap. (Dúchas, the Heritage Service)

33

*Photo 14
Abernethy
(Perthshire,
Scotland). One
of two Irish
style towers in
Scotland (the
other is at
Brechin, Angus).
The quality of
the masonry and
the Romanesque
details indicate
a twelfth-century
date.*

ORIGINS AND INFLUENCES

Most scholars believe that the Irish round tower must have derived from prototypes abroad. There are depictions of round towers in ivories and manuscript illuminations, both European and Byzantine, from the sixth century onwards, but none appear to be based on specific monuments. In Italy, southern France and Catalonia, detached towers became a common feature from the late tenth century, as part of the style that is known as 'first Romanesque', but the towers in this case were square in plan and the walls were opened out with large windows. There are several circular towers in Ravenna but these towers are built of brick, have large windows, and lack conical roofs; furthermore they are thought to date from the eleventh century at the earliest, post-dating the introduction of the towers to Ireland (Pl 15). Circular towers are otherwise rare in Italy, though there is of course the famous twelfth-century 'leaning tower' at Pisa.

The Irish towers, with their circular form, raised doorways and conical caps, are distinctive. There are three similar towers outside Ireland, one on the Isle of Man and two in Scotland (Photo 14), but these appear to be modelled on the Irish examples.

Round towers were also known in Anglo-Saxon England. A belfry at York was described in 801 as *domus clocarum* or 'house of bells', a phrase which is suspiciously close to the Irish term *cloigtheach*, 'bell house'.

The overall picture is thus extremely confused, and for the time being the origin of the Irish round tower remains an open question.

It is not clear which Irish monastery or settlement was responsible for building the first round tower. The general consistency of the architectural form suggests that there was a prestigious exemplar, which served as a prototype for the early builders. Such a prototype was presumably to be found at one of the more influential monastic establishments – Kildare, Clonmacnoise, Kells or Armagh perhaps.

The annals provide a few hints. A majority of the references to round towers in the tenth and eleventh centuries relate to places in the north and east of the country; in fact four of the first five entries are linked to establishments associated with St Patrick or Armagh (Slane, Louth, Armagh twice, and Down). Admittedly this may only reflect the origin of the annals themselves, but if one was forced to choose, Armagh is a plausible candidate. There was certainly a round tower there by 995–6,

35

which may have preceded that at Slane. The construction of the first circular belfry, 100 feet high, would have been a dramatic innovation that would have accorded well with Armagh's claims to jurisdiction over all the churches of Ireland.

CONSTRUCTION FEATURES

Height and proportions

There are approximately twenty-six towers where the height is either known or can be calculated with reasonable accuracy. The heights vary quite considerably: the tallest surviving tower (34m) is to be found at Kilmacduagh (Photo 10, Pl 11), though it was once exceeded by that at Fertagh where the top is now ruined (Photo 15). If one excludes a group of three relatively low towers (Dromiskin, Castledermot and Turlough), the average height is 29.53 metres, a dimension that is equivalent to 97 English feet or 100 Roman feet. Averages of course can be misleading and many towers differ quite significantly from this dimension. But it does raise the possibility that Irish churchmen expected their towers to be in the order of 100 feet high.

The circumferences vary from 13.10 to 17.86 metres, with a high proportion clustering around the average of 15.63 metres, or 51 feet 3 inches (close to half the average height). This suggests – though it is difficult to prove this – the existence of a formula ordaining that the height of a round tower should be approximately twice its circumference.

This was certainly the case at Glendalough, where the tower is 100 feet high (30.48 metres), and 50 feet 2 inches (15.30 metres) in circumference at the base (Photo 2). This is unlikely to be a coincidence.

The simple ratio of 1:2 between circumference and height might have been regarded as a way of ensuring stability, but the idea of a 100 foot tower also invites symbolical interpretations. As a perfect number, 100 is frequently cited in both the Old and New Testaments, and the same figure is often mentioned in Early Christian commentaries. We shall probably never know, however, exactly how the abbot and his builders established the dimensions of their towers.

Corbelled roofs

The corbelled roofs, described in the annals as *bennchobbor*, constructed 100 feet above the ground, were no mean feats of engineering (Photos 2, 3, 16). Masonry caps were virtually unknown in Europe before the development of the stone spire in the twelfth century. Early Romanesque towers usually had roofs of lead, tiles or stone slates, built over a wooden frame.

Photo 16 Kilmacduagh (Galway). A view looking up into the conical cap, showing the corbelled system used in construction, a technique with a long history in Ireland. (Dúchas, The Heritage Service)

The annals contain six references to towers being damaged by lightning or thunderbolts, a danger to which towers were exceedingly vulnerable. There are two references in the annals, in 995 and 1015, relating to Armagh and Down, to towers being *burned* by lightning. All subsequent references, however, are to caps being split or knocked off. In 1134, for example, the annals report that 'lightning knocked off the head of the steeple of Cluain-muc-Nois', the head presumably referring to the capstone of the fine tower which had been completed only eleven years before.

In other words, fire seems to have been a factor only in the early cases. From this one might deduce that the first towers had wooden roofs, and that the introduction of the stone roof was an attempt to reduce the dangers. The stone roof may also have improved the acoustics, increasing the resonance of the bells.

37

Vulnerability to wind

As well as the threat from lightning, towers were also vulnerable to high winds. 'Many steeples' were said to have been destroyed in the storms of 981 and 1137, and the tower at Ross Carbery blew down in 1285. Under the year 1039 the annals report that the tower at Clonard 'fell down to the earth', and another tower collapsed at Ardbraccan in 1181.

Although the circular form of the towers made them inherently quite strong, Irish builders failed to realise the importance of deep foundations; in some cases the masonry descends less than two or three feet below ground level. Moreover, some towers were built, unwittingly, over graves, which meant that they were vulnerable to differential settlement, with one side sinking further into the ground. This probably explains the 'lean' at Kilmacduagh (Photo 10, Pl 11). When human bones were discovered at the base of some towers in the nineteenth century, it led to the mistaken belief that the towers were designed as elongated mausolea.

Photo 17 Rattoo (Kerry). A well constructed tower where the batter is very subtle. Apart from the belfry stage there is only one window, so clambering up the ladders inside the tower must have been a hazardous undertaking. (Dúchas, The Heritage Service)

Tapering profile

Another intriguing feature of the towers is the tapering profile, which varies quite considerably from tower to tower. At Rattoo the diameter of the tower is reduced by almost a quarter (Photo 17). At Glendalough the reduction is more gentle, though it is still sufficient to give the tower a certain life and elasticity (Photo 2). At Clonmacnoise the batter on the west side of the tower is quite acute until the level of the doorway, at which point there appears to have been a change in alignment (Pl 2).

It is quite rare to find diminution of this sort elsewhere in early medieval Europe.

*Photo 18 Ardmore
(Waterford).
One of the finest
towers, built with
excellent ashlar
masonry and
Romanesque
details. String
courses divide the
tower into four
clear stages; the
diminution or
batter is more
extravagant here
than in any other
tower. (Dúchas,
The Heritage
Service)*

39

Photo 19 Scattery (Clare). The round tower of this island monastery, situated in the Shannon estuary, undergoing repairs in 1916. Scattery is one of only two towers where the doorway is at ground level (the other is at Castledermot). (Dúchas, The Heritage Service)

SCATTERY IS.   16·3·1916

40

Most circular towers on the continent are constructed as cylinders, and, if they were narrowed, this was usually achieved in a regular manner by the introduction of offsets, as at Ravenna (Pl 14). In Romanesque architecture such offsets were often marked by decorated string courses, which were introduced in some of the Irish twelfth-century towers.

Diminution and offsets were really alternatives, but at Ardmore the builders tried to get the best of both worlds, with string courses and an element of batter (Photo 18). In this case the narrowing is pronounced and irregular: indeed, the tower is almost two metres narrower at the top than at the bottom.

The gradual reduction in width must have been quite difficult to control and it made it difficult for builders to use plumb lines to test the verticality of the towers. Clearly, diminution mattered, but what was its purpose? As well as improving the look of the tower, it did have some structural value, an equivalent to the inclined jambs found on so many lintelled doorways. As such it may have been founded on constructional beliefs stretching far back into Irish pre-history.

Construction methods

Putlog holes at several towers show that they were erected with external scaffolding, perhaps not dissimilar to that used by the Board of Works when repairing the tower on Scattery Island in the years around 1916 (Photo 19).

The lifting of stone to heights in excess of 100 feet was without precedent in Ireland, and must have demanded considerable mechanical expertise in the use of pulleys and hoists. On the basis of the distribution of the putlog holes, one writer has calculated that a tower could have been erected in seven or eight months; whether true or not, the introduction of the round tower represented a technological, as well as an architectural, milestone in Irish society.

*Photo 20
O'Meara's Irish
House, Dublin
(1870).
Surmounting a
battery of
nationalist
symbols (which
include
wolfhounds,
methers, and a
grieving Érin),
The pub was
crowned by a line
of towers,
arranged like
fortified turrets
(Edwin Smith).*

A NATIONAL ICON

By establishing the historical context of the towers, and by confirming their religious and moral respectability, Petrie's book of 1845 helped to give the round tower a new lease of life as a symbol of Irish nationalism. During the second half of the nineteenth century, the round tower joined the wolfhound, the shamrock, and the Irish harp as a national emblem.

It found favour with a number of publicans and there was a famous drinking establishment in Dublin, now destroyed, in which a line of six round towers was silhouetted on the skyline (Photo 20). At Listowel in County Kerry a round tower, painted appropriately in green, takes its place alongside a buxom Érin over the doorway to the Central Hotel (Pl 16a). Architects like James Franklin Fuller were keen to incorporate round towers into their compositions and they began to spring up as adjuncts to new churches and even country houses (Pl 16c).

A massive round tower was constructed to celebrate the achievements of Daniel O'Connell in Glasnevin cemetery, a truly heroic version of the ancient form, fifty feet higher than any of its medieval predecessors (Pl 16b). Another tower was erected at Ferrycarrig (Wexford) as a memorial to those who died in the Crimean war. Even today the round tower retains an association with fallen heroes. In 1998 a tower on the ancient model was constructed at Messines in Belgium to commemorate those Irish soldiers who died during the first world war.

Photo 21 Kilrea (Kilkenny). The tower built of well coursed masonry lies a short distance from the famous high cross, its surfaces embellished with abstract ornament.

Photo 22 Turlough (Mayo). One of the shortest towers, with a capstone that was rather clumsily repaired in the nineteenth century. Little is known about the ecclesiastical settlement here; long before the tower was built St Patrick is said to have baptised many people in the local well.

44

Photo 23
A comment on the
round tower from
Martyn Turner,
Illuminations,
101 Drawings
from Early
Irish History
(Kilkenny
1985/6).
(Reproduced by
kind permission
of Martyn Turner)

45

SELECT BIBLIOGRAPHY

Petrie, G, *The Ecclesiastical Architecture of Ireland. An essay on the origin and uses of the round towers of Ireland* (Dublin, 1845, reprinted Shannon, 1970)

Stokes, M, *Early Christian Architecture in Ireland* (London, 1878)

Champneys, A, *Irish Ecclesiastical Architecture* (London, 1910), 48–62

Barrow, GL, *The Round Towers of Ireland* (Dublin, 1979) – contains a valuable gazetteer, but not to be trusted on historical issues

Rynne, E, 'The Round Towers of Ireland –a review article', *North Munster Antiquarian Journal*, XXII (1980), 27–32

Bourke, C, 'Early Irish Hand-Bells', *Journal of the Royal Society of Antiquaries of Ireland*, 110 (1980), 52–66

Sheehy, J, *The Rediscovery of Ireland's Past: The Celtic Revival 1830–1930* (London, 1980).

Hare, M and Hamlin, A, 'The study of early church architecture in Ireland: an Anglo-Saxon viewpoint, with an appendix on documentary evidence for round towers', in *The Anglo-Saxon Church, papers on history, architecture, and archaeology in honour of Dr H.M.Taylor*, ed by LAS Butler and RK Morris, (London, Council for British Archaeology, 1986), pp 131–45

McDonnell, H, 'Margaret Stokes and the Irish Round Tower: A Reappraisal', *Ulster Journal of Archaeology*, 57 (1994), 70–80

Manning, C, 'The Date of the Round Tower at Clonmacnoise', *Archaeology Ireland*, volume 11, number 2 (summer 1997), 12–13

O'Reilly, S, 'Birth of a Nation's Symbol: the Revival of Ireland's Round Towers', *Irish Arts Review Yearbook*, volume 15 (1999), 27–33

Lalor, B, *The Irish Round Tower, Origins and Architecture Explored* (Cork, 1999)

Stalley, RA, 'Sex, Symbol and Myth: some observations on the Irish round towers', in *From Ireland, Coming*, edited by C Hourihane (Princeton, 2000)

OTHER TITLES IN THE SERIES:

The Bend of the Boyne (Geraldine Stout, 1997)

Crannogs: Lake-dwellings in Early Ireland (Aidan O'Sullivan, 2000)

*****Early Celtic Art in Ireland** (Eamonn P Kelly, 1993)

*****Early Irish Communion Vessels** (Michael Ryan, 2000)

Early Irish Monasteries (Conleth Manning, 1995)

Exploring the Burren (George Cunningham, 1998)

*****The Fenians** (Michael Kenny, 1994)

Irelands Archaeology from the Air (Tom Condit, 1997)

Irish Castles and Fortified Houses (David Sweetman, 1995)

*****Irish Furniture and Woodcraft** (John Teahan, 1994)

Irish Prehistory: An Introduction (Anna Brindley, 1995)

Irish Shrines and Reliquaries of the Middle Ages (Raghnall Ó Flionn, 1994)

Irish Wrecks of the Spanish Armada (Laurence Flanagan, 1995)

Megalithic Art in Ireland (Muiris O'Sullivan, John Scarey, 1993)

Metal Craftsmanship in Early Ireland (Michael Ryan, 1993)

*****The Road to Freedom** (Michael Kenny, 1993)

*****The 1798 Rebellion** (Michael Kenny, 1996)

*****Sheela-na-Gigs** (Eamonn P Kelly, 1996)

Stone Circles in Ireland (Seán Ó Nualláin, 1995)

Walled Towns in Ireland (John Bradley, 1995)

Where Has Ireland Come From? (Frank Mitchell, 1994)

Published by Country House in association with the National Museum of Ireland